CHRISTIAN LEADERSHIP

by Peter Mansell

Contents

I.S.B.N. 0 947778 12 8

Publications of The Open Bible Trust must be in accordance with the evangelical, fundamental and dispensational basis of the Trust. However, beyond this minimum, writers are free to express whatever beliefs they may have as their own personal understanding, provided that the aim in so doing is to further the object of the Trust. A copy of the doctrinal basis is available from:—

THE OPEN BIBLE TRUST,
36 Hardwick Road,
Reading, RG3 4LN, U.K.

Christian Leadership

1 Introduction

1.1 What is leadership?

Leadership plays a part in almost every activity of human life. Consequently, definitions of leadership are many and varied.
Here are just a few:

> *Leadership* is the capacity and will to rally men and women to a common purpose.
>
> *Leadership* is the power of one man to influence another.
>
> *Leadership* is the ability to recognise the special abilities and limitations of each individual combined with the ability to fit each one into the job where he will do his best.

It can be seen that the common theme which links these definitions is that leadership exists in circumstances where two or more people are involved in jointly trying to achieve a task. Leadership comes into play where you have a team of people working together towards a common objective.

One might object and say that these definitions are carnal and not spiritual. Is the concept of leadership ordained by God? We will see that the concept of leadership permeates the Scriptures. For instance, in Romans 12:6-8 we read:

> 'We have different gifts, according to the grace given us . . . if it is leadership, let him govern diligently . . .'

It also appears that the spiritual realms involve some form of hierarchy for we read in 1 Peter 3:22:

> '(Jesus Christ) Who has gone into heaven and is at God's right hand — with angels, authorities and powers in submission to Him.'

Similarly, in 1 Thessalonians 4:16 and Jude 9 there are references to an archangel, i.e. a first or chief angel, indicating that some angels have more authority than others.

We can state, therefore, that leadership is not contrary to the plan of God for His people. However, as with many of man's natural attributes, leadership can be used for good or evil. It is the duty of Christian leaders to ensure that leadership talents are blended with spiritual attributes so as to raise those talents to their highest effectiveness in God's service; remembering that the aim of Christian leadership is not to be the master but the servant.

> 'For even the Son of Man did not come to be served, but to serve, and to give His life as a ransom for many.' (Mark 10:44)

1.2 Why is leadership necessary?

Men and women, working together in unison, are capable of joint achievements far beyond those they can achieve as individuals. To work together in unison somebody must be exercising leadership; objectives need to be agreed and communicated, decisions need to be taken, tasks need to be allocated, discipline needs to be enforced and enthusiasm needs to be generated. In other words, good leadership enables a group of individuals to work together to their full potential.

The Scriptures record God's own testimonial to the effectiveness of a group of people working together in unison. In Genesis 11 we read of the building of the tower of Babel. On seeing the tower, the Lord said:

> 'If as one people speaking the same language they have begun to do this, then nothing they plan to do will be impossible for them.'

To dilute this power, God found it necessary to confuse the languages of men. But that power of itself is not evil and can and should be harnessed by Christian leaders in God's service.

One of our definitions of leadership was 'the power of one man to influence another.' This power of leadership is amply illustrated in the history of the people of Israel. Time and time again we read in the books of Judges and Kings of how the moral state of the whole nation was influenced by the leader of the nation. Similarly, in the history of the Church, God has raised up men of influence to lead Christians back to God; men like Luther, Calvin and Wesley.

The Scriptures also spell out the tragedy of a situation in which people are left without effective leadership. For instance, in Mark 6:34 we read:

> 'When Jesus landed and saw a large crowd, He had compassion on them, because they were like sheep without a shepherd. So He began teaching them many things.'

The Lord is here echoing the feelings of Moses, who was also concerned about the lack of leadership in Israel. In the case of Moses, his concern was for a successor when the Lord announced to him that he was about to die.

> 'Moses said to the Lord, "May the Lord the God of the spirits of all mankind, appoint a man over this community to go out and come in before them, one who will lead them out and bring them in, so that the Lord's people will not be like sheep without a shepherd." '

Leadership by effective and caring shepherds is necessary to help bring individuals to their full potential in God's service and to ensure that the people of God are protected and kept from aimless wandering.

1.3 Who should be concerned about leadership?

The quality of the leadership in any group affects every member of the group. Therefore every Christian should be concerned to be able to recognise and encourage good leadership even if they are not directly involved in providing that leadership.

There is a tendency to believe that it is necessary for only one person to exercise leadership in a group. However, as we have observed, leadership involves influencing others and that is best achieved through personal contact. In all but the smallest groups there is a need for people to exercise leadership in many areas and at many levels. Moses was taught this important lesson by his father-in-law.

> 'When his father-in-law saw all that Moses was doing for the people he said "What is this you are doing for the people? Why do you alone sit as judge while all these people stand round you from morning till evening?" . . . . . Moses listened to his father-in-law and did everything he said. He chose capable men from all Israel and made them leaders of the people over thousands, hundreds, fifties and tens.' (Exodus 18:14-24)

There is a need today for more Christians to be taking an active part in leadership. An individual may not be called upon to lead a congregation of two hundred believers but his talents might be needed to lead a small prayer or study group which, together with several other groups, will cover the whole congregation.

Some may be reluctant to become involved in Christian leadership because they are wary of being seen to desire the honour and prestige that accompany a position of authority. This is a danger but, on the other hand, it is equally incorrect to be falsely modest and not to use the talents the Lord has given. Paul wrote to Timothy:

> 'Here is a trustworthy saying: If anyone sets his heart on being an overseer, he desires a noble task.' (1 Timothy 3:1)

Those already in positions of Christian leadership need to recognise their responsibility, as with Moses, to involve others in the ministry of leadership. Not only should they be concerned themselves to progress as leaders but they must also spend time encouraging and training others. The Lord Jesus Christ spent a significant part of His earthly ministry in training the twelve apostles. Similarly, Paul worked with Timothy as a father with his son to train him as an effective Christian leader.

2 Church Government

2.1 Biblical Guidelines

The Scriptures and human experience declare the necessity of good leadership. Does the Bible lay down any conditions or guidelines as to the structure that leadership should have?

Today some churches have an elaborate 'pyramid' type of leadership structure with a supreme leader and then various levels of cardinals, bishops, vicars, priests, curates, deacons etc. Other churches stress the autonomy of the local congregation based around a board of elders and a pastor. Do the Scriptures define a specific structure for church government or are we free to select a structure to suit our own circumstances?

Looking at God's people in the Old Testament, we find that Israel was a highly organised community in its civil and its religious life. Although the civil and the religious sometimes overlapped, there were distinct structures for civil affairs and for religious affairs. These two leadership structures were typified by the distinction between Moses and his brother Aaron. Moses was the law-maker, the prophet and the judge, but he was not the ceremonial priest who made acceptable sacrifice before God for the people of Israel. This rôle was reserved for Aaron.

These two authorities in Israel developed separately. The priestly order was vested in the descendents of Aaron. The civil law became the responsibility of those termed as *elders*. The office of elder had existed in Israel prior to the time of Moses, for example see Exodus 3:16, but, under the Law God gave through Moses, the elders acquired particular duties in Israel. For instance, we read in Leviticus 4:13,14:

> 'If the whole Israelite community sins unintentionally and does what is forbidden in any of the Lord's commands, even though the community is unaware of the matter, they are guilty. When they become aware of the sin they committed, the assembly must bring a young bull as a sin offering and present it before the Tent of Meeting. The elders of the community are to lay their hands on the bull's head before the Lord, and the bull shall be slaughtered before the Lord.'

Not only did Israel have a national assembly of elders (1 Kings 8:1) but each city had its assembly of elders (Deuteronomy 19:12). These institutions of government survived throughout the periods of the Judges and the Kings and even into the captivity (Ezra 10:8).

The office of elder was still in existence in the Lord's time but the separate office of priest seems to have become intertwined with civil government, especially in the Jewish ruling council, the Sanhedrin (Matthew 26:57-59).

2.2 The Apostolic Church

The death and resurrection of the Lord Jesus Christ is the central point of human history. Jesus Christ, the only perfect man, was immune to the law of sin and death, yet at Calvary He laid down His life voluntarily and, bearing our sins on that cross, became a ransom for many. Three days later, as He had predicted, He rose from the dead, the firstborn of a new creation. God manifest in the flesh had broken the power of sin and death not just for Himself but for all those who put their trust in the Sacrifice He has made.

These momentous events had two implications for the organisation of Christ's disciples. First, the intermediary role of human priests was no longer necessary 'because Jesus lives for ever, He has a permanent priesthood. Therefore He is able so save completely those who come to God through Him, because He always lives to intercede for them' (Hebrews 7:24,25). The role fulfilled by Aaron and his descendents as representing the people before God was no longer necessary because Jesus Christ had opened up a direct channel to God for everyone.

Secondly, the number of believers started to grow dramatically. There were only about 120 disciples before Pentecost, but about three thousand were added to their number in one day alone (Acts 1:15, 2:41).

It was in this environment of a new spiritual equality and dramatic growth in numbers that the apostolic church began to organise itself. The resulting organisation has formed the basis for many peoples' ideas as to how Christian communities should structure themselves today. However, it is not easy to identify the exact meaning and relevance of all the positions of authority mentioned, which include apostles, elders, bishops, deacons, pastors, teachers, prophets and evangelists. How did all these offices fit together within the early Christian communities?

(a) Apostle

The word apostle comes to us straight from the Greek word *apostolos* meaning a messenger. The title of apostle is restricted to a very select group in Scripture. The Lord commissioned only twelve apostles during His earthly ministry. These apostles, as the number twelve suggests, were associated particularly with the twelve tribes of Israel. Later, as one born out of due time, the Lord commissioned Paul, or Saul as he then was, as an apostle or messenger to the Gentiles.

The key aspect of an apostle as someone *sent* with a message from God is brought out in both the selection of the twelve:

> 'Jesus went up into the hills and called to Him those He wanted, and they came to Him. He appointed twelve — designating them apostles — that they might be with Him and that He might *send* them out to preach' (Mark 3:13,14),

and Paul:

> 'I will rescue you from your own people and the Gentiles.
>
> I am *sending* you to open their eyes. . . . .' (Acts 26:17.18)

These apostles were *sent* with a message direct from Jesus Christ and that message revolved around what they had seen or been shown by Jesus Christ and as such theirs was a unique ministry.

Some expositors doubt whether the title Apostle can truly be used in the same sense of anyone other than Paul and the twelve. However, Barnabas, James the Lord's brother, Andronicus and Junias are mentioned in Scripture as apostles, but possibly in a wider sense of the word messenger as, say, missionaries, (Acts 14:14, Galatians 1:19 and Romans 16:7).

The Apostles' role was essentially foundational in that they were commissioned to spread their message from God in much the same way as the Old Testament Prophets. Although they did exercise authority and act as overseers this was not their prime function or their sole responsibility. We read in Acts 15:6 that the Council at Jerusalem was composed of elders as well as apostles. Also, we shall see that the role of governing was usually given to local elders rather than the missionary apostles.

Paul and the twelve had a unique ministry which is obviously not repeated today. The nearest we have to the role of apostle today is that of the missionary involved in founding new churches and providing a model of Christian practice where none has previously existed.

(b) Elders

We have already seen that the role of elder, as a sort of town councillor, was well established in Israel. The term does imply someone of above average age but it is clear that age was not the only criteria; being wise and respected were equally important (Deuteronomy 1:15). This idea of government by elders was not unique to Israel for in Roman and Arab societies the words senator and sheikh have elder as their root meaning.

It seems likely that the early Christians carried the practice of government by elders over into the Church from either civil government or from the synagogue, where elders also formed a ruling council. The earliest reference to a Christian community being governed by elders is at Jerusalem (Acts 11:30). Paul and Barnabas appointed elders in Lystra, Iconium and Antioch (Acts 14:23) and Titus was instructed to appoint elders in every town in Crete (Titus 1:5). It therefore appears very likely that this was the normal practice in the early Church, i.e. each Christian community had a council of elders responsible for order and good government.

(c) Bishops

The word translated as bishop in the Authorised Version is the Greek word *episkopos*. The word occurs, in its various forms, eleven times in Scripture and in a modern translation, such as the New International Version, is rendered as *overseer*.

In Acts 20:17 and 28 the same group of people are referred to as elders and overseers (bishops) respectively. Similarly, in Titus 1:5-9 the two titles are seemingly used interchangeably. Consequently, it appears likely that overseer is simply used as another title referring to the office of elder, the term being descriptive of the role actually being performed. Certainly there is nothing in Scripture to indicate the existence of bishops as superior members of some form of full-time religious hierarchy. This modern idea of bishops was only introduced into the Church in the early second century A.D..

(d) Deacons

The word deacon is a literal rendering of the Greek word *diakonos* which generally means a servant. *Diakonos,* together with the words derived from it, is a common word in Scripture occurring 100 times. Outside of the Scriptures the word is often used for somebody who waits on tables and it is used in this sense in John 2:5, referring to the servants at the wedding in Cana. In Scripture the word is used in a broader sense as a helper or attendant or someone who ministers to others' needs.

The idea that some members of the early church were specifically designated as helpers (deacons) is derived from Philippians 1:1 and 1 Timothy 3:1-12. The implication of both these passages is that congregations were organised on a similar model to synagogues, where not only were there councils of elders but also official attendants (see Luke 4:20). Also, in view of the administration involved in any human organisation, it does not seem unreasonable to suggest that early Christian congregations would have had official helpers (deacons).

Acts 6:1-7 records the selection of seven men whose responsibilities were to include waiting at table. These seven are consequently often referred to as deacons. However, it is interesting to note that Philip, one of the seven, is later referred to as an evangelist and Stephen, whose martyrdom is recorded in Acts 7, obviously had a calling which extended beyond being an *attendant*.

There is a sense in which we all serve or minister to the needs of others, we are all deacons even if we do not serve in the restricted sense of assisting church elders.

(e) Pastors

The Greek word *poimen* is usually translated as shepherd in all its occurrences except for Ephesians 4:11, where it is rendered as pastor. However, it is clear that in this passage the idea of shepherding is intended rather than a new office in the church. As with the title overseer, pastor or shepherd is descriptive of the work actually being performed by an elder. For instance, we read in Acts 20:28 Paul's instructions to the Ephesian elders:

> 'Keep watch over yourselves and all the flock of which the Holy Spirit has made you overseers. Be shepherds of the church of God, which He bought with His own blood.'

Thus, being a pastor or shepherd is just one facet of the work of an elder and does not denote a separate office.

(f) Teachers, Prophets and Evangelists

In the New Testament we read of various individuals who were known as teachers, prophets or evangelists. Acts 13:1 names five individuals in the church at Antioch who were prophets or teachers or perhaps both. Similarly, Acts 15:32 names Judas and Silas as prophets in the church at Jerusalem, as was Agabus (Acts 11:27,28). There are, by comparison, fewer references to evangelists although, as we have noted above, Philip is described as an evangelist in Acts 21:8.

These people obviously played an important part in the early church and presumably received their titles because they were particularly gifted at either teaching or proclaiming God's word or preaching the gospel. However, there is no indication that those gifted in these ways were necessarily involved in the government of their Christian communities.

In summary, we can see that the general pattern of government in the early Christian communities was for a group of elders to oversee and shepherd the congregation. They were supported in this work by individuals gifted in teaching and prophecy and by specific helpers or deacons. A general pastoral care was also supplied by the foundational apostles and their missionary assistants such as Titus and Timothy.

In conclusion, we must not forget that above these human positions of authority, all are subject to the Lord Jesus Christ. Not only is He our Lord and Head but He is also the perfect example of each of the offices we have considered. He is the great:

Apostle (Hebrews 3:1)
Shepherd and Overseer (1 Peter 2:25)
Servant or Deacon (Romans 15:8)
Teacher (John 3:2)
Prophet (Luke 1:76) and
Preacher of the Gospel (Luke 20:1)

2.3 What form of church government is appropriate today?

The prime office of leadership in the local congregations of the early church was that of the elder or overseer. However, the Scriptures do not declare that this is the only true and acceptable method of governing a group of believers. Our circumstances today are different from those of the early church. We no longer have Apostles to provide the ultimate oversight. Instead we have a complete Bible which provides principles and examples for our guidance.

In many congregations today the real authority does not lie with a council of elders but with a vicar or pastor. This can lead to the idea that the church is under the authority of a revised form of the Old Testament priesthood, where one man or group of men undertakes all the spiritual functions of the congregation. This is not the model which the Scriptures provide as to the workings of the Church. In Scripture the congregation of Christians is likened to a body:

> 'Just as each of us has one body with many members, and these members do not all have the same function, so in Christ we who are many form one body and each member belongs to all the others' (Romans 12:4,5).

Thus the crux of the matter is not so much as to whether government is exercised by one person or a group of people but that every member of the congregation is being involved in the work of the congregation. All believers do not have the same gifts and we are brought back to the importance of leadership as specified in one of our original definitions, '*leadership* is the ability to recognise the special abilities and limitations of each individual combined with the ability to fit each one into the job where he will do his best.'

There is a clear Scriptural precedent for government by a council of elders. They may call themselves overseers, bishops, elders, pastors or anything else appropriate but they must ensure that the necessary leadership is provided for 'the flock over which God has made them overseers.'

3 Selection of Christian Leaders

3.1 Character

It used to be a widely held belief that leadership ability was a sort of innate superiority. Either you had it or you didn't and, if you didn't, there was no way you could acquire it. Then there was a move to the opposite view that anybody could become a leader if properly trained. The truth, as usual, lies somewhere in the middle of these two extremes.

Paul, in his advice to Timothy and Titus, points out a number of character weaknesses which would make a person ineligible for a position of Christian leadership. These include being quick-tempered, overbearing, violent, quarrelsome and being given to much wine or to dishonest gain (1 Timothy 3:2-12; Titus 1:6-9).

There are at least three reasons why Paul's advice is as appropriate today as it was then. First, those in positions of responsibility must exemplify the Christian way of life; if they fail in this due to some character weakness, such as violence or drunkenness, they bring the whole congregation, not just themselves, into disrepute. Paul confirms this when he says that an overseer 'must also have a good reputation with outsiders', (1 Timothy 3:7).

Secondly, a glaring character weakness gives the Devil an opportunity. It represents a chink in the Christian's armour. For example, Judas Iscariot was given to dishonest gain. He helped himself to the disciples' communal money bag, and Satan exploited this to the end that Judas was eventually prepared to sell even the Lord of Life for thirty pieces of silver.

Thirdly, people will only follow somebody they respect. If a potential leader is, say, overbearing he will not be able to command the respect of those he is supposed to lead and his leadership will be ineffective.

Paul sums this up under the headings of being blameless or above reproach; asking of someone, 'Does he have a good reputation and the respect of those who know him both within and outside the congregation?' However, the character of a potential Christian leader must also include certain key positive attributes.

(a) Humility

This is the supreme attribute required of the Christian leader. It was said of Moses that he 'was a very humble man, more humble than anyone else on the face of the earth' (Numbers 12:3). This is not the false humility of a Uriah Heap but the humility that led John the Baptist to say 'He (the Lord Jesus Christ) must become greater; I must become less' (John 3:30). It is the humility that led Paul to think of himself as the least of the apostles, then, the least of all God's people, and finally, the worst of sinners (1 Corinthians 15:9, Ephesians 3:8, 1 Timothy 1:15).

It is flattering to be entrusted with authority. Consequently, the potential Christian leader must be fully aware that Christian leadership is about washing the feet of the saints (John 13:5), not lording it over them.

(b) Courage

In apostolic times, and in some parts of the world today, Christian leadership has led to martyrdom. This form of physical courage may, thankfully, not be called upon for most Christian leaders but moral courage certainly is required. Paul had to remind even Timothy that God does not give us a spirit of timidity (2 Timothy 1:7) and to tell Titus that he should encourage and rebuke with all authority, letting no one despise him (Titus 2:15). Also, when Joshua took on the responsibility of leadership for the people of Israel, the Lord told him three times to be strong and courageous.

> 'Do not be terrified, do not be discouraged for the Lord your God will be with you wherever you go.' (Joshua 1:9)

There can be no greater example of courage for the Christian leader than that of the Lord Jesus Christ. Not only was He willing to endure the pain and humiliation of the cross but much more than this, He was prepared to bear our sins and to be forsaken by His Father (Matthew 27:46).

(c) A Wise and Discerning Heart

The Lord appeared to Solomon and told him 'Ask for whatever you want Me to give you' (1 Kings 3:5). In reply, Solomon acknowledged that he did not know how to carry out his duties as king over such a great number of people and so he asked for a discerning heart. We read that God was pleased to give Solomon a wise and discerning heart and also added the riches and honour that Solomon had not asked for, (1 Kings 3:10-14).

A Christian leader will be faced with decisions about all sorts of people and situations. To command respect both within and outside the congregation he will need to display wisdom and discernment in handling these situations. Consequently, a Christian leader must be a man of proven judgment.

(d) Self-discipline

Paul advised Timothy and Titus that an overseer should be self-controlled and disciplined. He also described to the Corinthians the singleness of purpose required from each Christian in the field in which they were called to serve (1 Corinthians 9:24-27).

To be effective a leader must be very conscious of his purpose, his objectives, and must have the perseverance to stick to that purpose avoiding the many distractions which will come along. Again, we have no better example than the Lord Jesus Christ. He set His face towards Jerusalem knowing what death He would suffer there but looking to the time when He would be able to cry, 'It is finished', (Matthew 16:21, John 19:30).

(e) Hospitable

Paul also advised Timothy and Titus that an overseer should be hospitable. This involves being welcoming and taking a genuine interest in people. Hospitality is a practical way of demonstrating care for other people. In Luke 7:36-50 we read that the Lord Jesus was invited to dinner by a Pharisee named Simon, but by a number of omissions Simon was not hospitable, thus demonstrating his lack of care.

A Christian leader must show concern for other people in a practical way. People soon sense whether they are liked and are welcome by the hospitality, or lack of it, that we extend towards them.

(f) Ability to Teach

Next to hospitality in 1 Timothy 3:2 we read that an overseer must have the ability to teach. Teaching ability is essentially about communication, being able to get across ideas and concepts. An outstanding example in Scripture is given by Nehemiah who set about organising the rebuilding of the walls of Jerusalem. His effectiveness in communicating the idea to the people is testified to by the record that 'they worked with all their heart', (Nehemiah 4:6).

This ability is measured by the effects it has on others, as with leadership as a whole. To be effective it is essential that a Christian leader be able to communicate ideas and concepts to those around him. There is a world of difference between being a good scholar and a good teacher, as many academics have found out to their cost.

3.2 Spiritual Maturity

It is not sufficient for a Christian leader just to have the sort of personality and talents outlined above. To be acceptable as a Christian leader that person must also display the correct attitude to both the Living and the Written Word of God.

A leader requires a strong motivation if he is going to succeed and that motivation must come from the love of the Lord Jesus Christ and awareness of our obligation to serve Him to the utmost of our ability. In Acts 6:3 we read that when the apostles required assistance in undertaking their responsibilities they specified that they should be 'full of the Spirit and wisdom.' Similarly, the apostle Paul was so motivated by his love for the Lord Jesus Christ that in his letters it is as if he can't go a few sentences without remarking on some wonderful aspect of his Lord.

A Christian leader must also have a firm grasp of Biblical doctrine. We read that he 'must keep hold of the deep truths of the faith with a clear conscience' and 'must hold firmly to the trustworthy message as it has been taught, so that he can encourage others by sound doctrine and refute those who oppose it' (1 Timothy 3:9 and Titus 1:9).

This familiarity with doctrine can be achieved only by constant reference to the Scriptures. In this context it is interesting to note in Deuteronomy 17:14-20 the decrees the Lord set out for the king that the Israelites would one day appoint over themselves. This involved the king in copying out by hand his own personal copy of the law which he was to keep with him and read all the days of his life. Similarly, the Lord commanded Joshua 'Do not let this Book of the Law depart from your mouth; meditate on it day and night, so that you may be careful to do everything written in it' (Joshua 1:8). It might be a lengthy process these days to write out the entire Bible by hand but a leader of a group of believers must be prepared to meditate on the Word such that he can say with David 'Your law is within my heart' (Psalm 40:8).

3.3 Tested

If an individual has the right attributes to become a leader and the necessary spiritual maturity he must still first be tested before he can serve

(1 Timothy 3:10). This is a general Scriptural principle for those who are going to serve God. The Lord Jesus Christ made it clear that 'Whoever can be trusted with very little can also be trusted with much' (Luke 16:10). Right at the start of His own public ministry the Lord was proved by being tested by Satan in the wilderness.

This principle is particularly important in the area of leadership, where too much authority should not be granted until an individual has proved himself in lesser tasks or in other areas of authority. For example, family life is itself a test of leadership for 'If anyone does not know how to manage his own family, how can he take care of God's church?' (1 Timothy 3:5). The apostle Paul also showed caution in appointing leaders. He warned Timothy not to be hasty in the laying on of hands, which was the traditional way of ceremonially conferring responsibility, and he waited until his second missionary journey before appointing elders in the churches founded in his first journey (1 Timothy 5:22 and Acts 14:23).

It may seem that with all these constraints the only people suitable for Christian leadership are those with tremendous talents and spotless virtue. However, if this were so, the Lord would not be able to use any of His human servants. With the exception of the Lord Jesus Christ, the Scriptures record the failings of even the greatest of leaders. Moses disobeyed the Lord at the waters of Meribah. David committed adultery and murder. Paul fell out with Barnabas over John Mark.

High standards are required for those who serve the Lord, but the Lord has not left us without a helper; as the Lord promised to be with Joshua so He is with those today who have responsibility in His Church. Nobody has all the desirable characteristics in full to be a Christian leader but, feeble as we are, the Lord still delights to use us.

4 Leadership Responsibilities

4.1 Responsibilities towards individuals

The prime responsibility of any leader of a group of Christians is to care for those individuals as a pastor or shepherd. Ephesians chapter four tells us that God has given men of ability to the Church 'to prepare God's people for works of service' (v.12) with the aim that each and every Christian should 'become mature, attaining to the whole measure of the fulness of Christ' (v.13).

In some congregations there is so much emphasis on the need for immediate evangelism that existing members of the congregation are not being built up. This is not to say that evangelism is not crucial to God's plan or that we could not do with more evangelists. However, those in positions of pastoral leadership are first obligated to the care of their existing flock, to feed each member by the Word of God and to help all to grow to maturity in Christ. Imagine the difference it would make to evangelism if each congregation had a majority of truly mature believers. This is God's ordained order that each Christian should grow and be trained and then they will be fit for all the necessary works of service, including evangelism and teaching others.

The first area in which Christian leaders are obligated to build up individual believers is in the knowledge of God as revealed in the Scriptures. The writer of Hebrews explained that we need to leave the elementary teachings and go on to maturity. An analogy is drawn between the believer's spiritual life and his natural life in that each believer must progress from infancy, when he can take only the milk of elementary truths, to maturity, when he can take the solid food of teaching about righteousness (Hebrews 5:11-6:3). Paul made a similar point when he said that those who are mature 'will no longer be infants tossed back and forth by waves and blown here and there by every wind of teaching' (Ephesians 4:14). Paul also made it clear to Timothy that it is the Scriptures which are the means of 'training in righteousness, so that the man of God may be thoroughly equipped for every good work' (2 Timothy 3:16,17) and that it was Timothy's responsibility to train others in sound doctrine (2 Timothy 2:2 and 4:2,3).

In any vocation, learning and progress are made only by a mixture of teaching and practice. The Christian leader, responsible for the development to maturity of his flock, must ensure that opportunities are taken to provide experience as well as teaching. The Lord Jesus Christ undertook the training of His disciples not just by giving them private tuition, as in the Sermon on the Mount (Matthew 5:1,2), but by sending them out to gain practical experience (Mark 6:7) and then discussing with them their experiences (Mark 6:30). This review of progress is a key part of the learning process. We know that the apostle Paul wrote open and frank letters to Timothy and Titus giving them encouragement and instruction. The same need for openness exists today at all levels of the Church.

Pastoral responsibility is not limited to teaching and training but involves the leader giving of himself in service for those under his care. The responsibility of the Christian leader towards individuals is essentially sacrificial. The success of this aspect of leadership is not judged by the eloquence and achievements of the leader but by the progress to maturity and the works of service of the congregation. This attitude was displayed by the apostle Paul in his letter to the Philippians, whom he described as his joy and crown (Philippians 4:1). Their growth to maturity was the proof of the success of his ministry:

> '. . . so that you may become blameless and pure, children of God without fault in a crooked and depraved generation, in which you shine like stars in the universe, as you hold out the word of life — in order that I may boast on the day of Christ that I did not run or labour for nothing.'

To achieve that growth Paul was prepared to give of himself:

> 'But even if I am being poured out like a drink offering on the sacrifice and service coming from your faith, I am glad and rejoice with all of you' (Philippians 2:15-17).

4.2 Responsibilities towards the group or congregation as a whole

It is well known in sport that a group of talented individuals does not of itself make a good team. The same is true in all fields of human endeavour, including the Church. It is necessary that Christian leaders recognise their responsibilities towards the congregation as a whole, not just towards individual members of the congregation.

(a) Providing 'vision'

One of our original definitions of leadership was 'the capacity and will to rally men and women to a common purpose.' For leadership to be effective that common purpose must be clearly defined and accepted by all members of the group. Working together with a shared objective then forms a bond between the members of the group to help overcome external opposition and the inevitable problems and disputes that arise even amongst Christians. This means that the leader must be very clear in his own mind and heart as to the direction in which the group is supposed to be going; in other words, he must be a man of vision.

We have already considered the impact that Nehemiah had on the people of Jerusalem when he provided them with the clear objective of rebuilding the city walls. Similarly, the Lord Jesus Christ caused amazement amongst the people of His time 'because He taught as one who had authority, and not as their teachers of the law' (Matthew 7:29).

Throughout secular as well as Christian history those who have had a clear idea of where they were going have united people in following the same path. The Christian leader also needs the same clear vision to help build unity in the congregation.

(b) Leading by example

The verb to lead means to go out in front. This means being visible so that others can follow, or *having a high profile.* No matter how effective a leader is as a speaker, if his words are not backed up by his actions people will not, and should not, follow his directions. It is often said, *Actions speak louder than words,* and this is particularly true in Christian leadership.

The Scriptures clearly teach that Christian leaders should be an example to those in their charge. The Lord Jesus Christ illustrated this aspect of His own leadership in a remarkable incident where He washed His disciples' feet, totally against the protocol of Jewish society. When He had finished the Lord explained 'Now that I, your Lord and Teacher, have washed your feet, you also should wash one another's feet. I have set you an example that you should do as I have done for you' (John 13:14,15). Peter passed on this message when he encouraged elders to be examples to the flock (1 Peter 5:3). Similarly, Paul exhorted the Corinthians 'Follow my example as I follow the example of Christ' (1 Corinthians 11:1). He also instructed Timothy to 'set an example for the believers in speech, in life, in love, in faith and in purity' (1 Timothy 4:12).

(c) Resolving disputes

Disputes and arguments are a significant threat to the unity of any group. We read in the Acts of the Apostles that when a dispute arose as to whether or not Gentile believers needed to be circumcised 'the apostles and elders met to consider this question' (Acts 15:6). It is essential that when a dispute arises, the leadership take action to resolve the dispute. If disputes are not dealt with they will escalate until they cause serious disharmony in the group.

Controversies sap energy and distract people from the main task in hand. It seems that the particular problem that plagued the early church was the position of Gentile believers with regard to the Law. Paul had to warn Titus and Timothy about avoiding foolish controversies, genealogies and arguments about the Law (Titus 3:9, 1 Timothy 1:4). The problems may be different today but the principle remains that unresolved controversies and disputes are divisive to the unity of a group of believers.

(d) Discipline

Discipline is an unfortunate necessity amongst a group of believers. In the Old Testament the Lord disciplined the people of Israel directly so as to purge the nation from sin, e.g. Numbers 21:4-9. Similarly, in the church of the Acts period, Ananias and Sapphira were struck down and 'great fear seized the whole church' (Acts 5:11). God may not move in direct judgment in this age of His grace but it is still true that the morale of the whole group will be destroyed if individual members are allowed to undermine the aims of the group.

Discipline, however, is a very powerful tool and requires experience and spiritual maturity if it is to be administered effectively. Part of the problem lies in the fact that with any group where membership is voluntary, the only discipline that can be enforced in the last resort is exclusion from the group. In this respect, Paul wrote to the Thessalonians:

> 'If anyone does not obey our instruction in this letter, take special note of him. Do not associate with him in order that he may feel ashamed. Yet do not regard him as an enemy, but warn him as a brother' (2 Thessalonians 3:15).

Unfortunately, expulsion from the fellowship of a group of believers has often been abused. Paul had to tell the Corinthians to reaffirm their love for a brother who had been disciplined (2 Corinthians 2:5-11) and advised Titus to warn a divisive person twice before having nothing to do with him (Titus 3:10). It should also be remembered that no church heirarchy, Christian leader or anyone else can separate a believer from the love of God that is in Christ Jesus our Lord (Romans 8:35-39).

In practical situations the circumstances in which a believer is excluded from fellowship, even for a short time, must be rare indeed. The more common course must be to follow Paul's advice to the Galatians:

> 'Brothers, if someone is caught in a sin, you who are spiritual should restore him gently. But watch yourself, or you also may be tempted.' (Galatians 6:1)

The aim in this situation is to speak the truth in love (Ephesians 4:15), although again this verse is easier to quote than to put into practice. Anyone considering 'speaking the truth in love' to another believer would be well advised to read 1 Corinthians 13 before they speak, remembering that 'No man can tame the tongue. It is a restless evil full of deadly poison' (James 3:8). Discipline and correction should be exercised only by mature believers and only after much thought and prayer.

(e) Encouragement

Discipline may be required from time to time, and should not be put off if it is necessary. However, most people will be more likely to be influenced by a word of encouragement. In general, positive reinforcement of what is good and desirable is a more effective training method than continual correction. The apostle Paul was always careful to encourage the progress made by a group of believers. For instance, he wrote to the Thessalonians:

> 'We ought always to thank God for you brothers, and rightly so, because your faith is growing more and more, and the love everyone of you has for each other is increasing. Therefore, among God's churches we boast about your perseverance and faith in all the persecutions and trials you are enduring.' (2 Thessalonians 1:3,4)

A distinction has to be drawn between flattery and encouragement, but where there is opportunity to give thanks for genuine progress that opportunity should be taken. This is an obligation on the Christian leader just as much as that of discipline, always remembering that both encouragement and discipline must be applied with absolute impartiality (1 Timothy 5:21).

4.3 Responsibilities towards the work

Christians are not in this world to be idle, 'For we are God's workmanship, created in Christ Jesus to do good works, which God prepared in advance for us to do' (Ephesians 2:10). The needs of the individual and the group must be balanced with the need to make progress with the work in hand.

Christian groups and congregations come in all forms and sizes, but all will be together to achieve some purpose or work, be it evangelism, Bible study, fellowship, caring for the aged and the sick, looking after widows and orphans or administration. The Christian leader takes first responsibility for the progress of the group. This means that the effective use of time by personal organisation is an important skill. We are all stewards of whatever the Lord has given us and that includes time. The effective use of time involves discipline and commitment, the discipline of a soldier or of an athlete training to win a race (2 Timothy 2:3-5).

No matter how effective a Christian leader is in the use of his time, there is a limit to how much can be achieved through his own endeavours. Sooner or later a Christian leader will need to delegate tasks to others. We have already considered the classic Scriptural example of delegation in Exodus 18 where, after listening to advice from his father-in-law, Moses delegated the simple cases to be judged by capable men, keeping the difficult cases for himself.

There are many reasons why some leaders are reluctant to delegate. Occasionally it is difficult to give up something which a leader has been in control of for many years. However, failure to delegate inevitably leads to a crisis when the leader becomes too old or too infirm to undertake the work he once did.

Delegation, like personal organisation, is a practical talent used in many areas of life, not just in a group of Christians. Like all aspects of Christian leadership it must be used in a sacrificial way. Responsible, interesting and challenging tasks must be delegated, not just the routine work.

It may seem that Christian leaders have a great weight of responsibility to bear with the needs of each individual, the needs of the group as a whole and the work of the group. This is often a heavy burden but the Christian leader can trust in the Lord Jesus Christ, Who said 'Come to Me all you who are weary and burdened, and I will give you rest' (Matthew 11:28).

5 Risks and Rewards of Christian Leadership

5.1 Leadership Risks

It is clear from Scripture that higher standards are demanded of those in positions of leadership. For instance, James wrote to the Jewish dispersion 'Not many of you should presume to be teachers, my brothers, because you know that we who teach will be judged more strictly' (James 3:1).

We know that each of us must one day give account to the Righteous Judge for our actions, and His reckoning will depend on the talents and responsibilities we have been given. The Lord Jesus made this clear in a number of His statements recorded in the gospels, such as 'From everyone who has been given much, much will be demanded; and from the one who has been entrusted with much, much more will be asked' (Luke 12:48). Consequently, during His earthy ministry, the Lord reserved His harshest words for the Pharisees and the rulers of the people.

Christian leadership is indeed a narrow walk. Not only are the responsibilities high but the Christian leader is exposed to a greater degree of trials and temptations. The greatest pitfall for a Christian leader is pride. Paul advised Timothy that an overseer 'must not be a recent convert, or he may become conceited and fall under the same judgment as the devil' (1 Timothy 3:6). A Christian is not eligible to be a leader unless he is respected, and this can so easily lead to pride, an inability to accept criticism and eventually to feelings of virtual infallibility. Christian leaders need to keep before them the record of Uzziah king of Judah 'His fame spread far and wide, for he was greatly helped until he became powerful. But after Uzziah became powerful, his pride led to his downfall' (2 Chronicles 26:15,16). 'The Lord detests all the proud of heart. Be sure of this; They will not go unpunished.' (Proverbs 16:5).

The leader must also be on his guard against the growth of a personality cult. This is a problem that has afflicted the Church ever since apostolic times. Dynamic and charismatic leaders can be very effective in God's service but there is always the danger that those who follow them are putting their trust in the leader and not in Jesus Christ. Paul had to give a strong warning to the church in Corinth about being 'followers of Paul' or 'followers of Apollos' (1 Corinthians 3:1-9). No leader is indispensable to God's service and leaders must make it clear that they are only servants (1 Corinthians 3:5), of no merit in themselves but only as channels of God's blessing.

Leadership confers authority and it is well established that power tends to corrupt even the most humble of men. The apostle Peter felt it necessary to warn elders not to 'lord it over those entrusted to them' (1 Peter 5:3). This risk of corruption together with the risk of pride result from the position of responsibility and are in addition to those temptations common to all men. The Christian leader needs, more than most, to put on the whole armour of God so that he can stand against the Devil's schemes (Ephesians 6:11).

5.2 Leadership costs

'Suppose one of you wants to build a tower. Will he not first sit down and estimate the cost to see if he has enough money to complete it?' (Luke 14:28). As with all forms of Christian service, leadership carries a potential cost which should be considered by those contemplating this form of service. In the early church those who held positions of leadership were often called upon to lay down their lives, to be faithful unto death as their Lord and Saviour had been. Paul recorded in 2 Corinthians 11:23-27 the physical sufferings he had endured as a result of his service for the churches. He was also to suffer rejection by those he had loved for we read in his last recorded letter 'At my first defence no-one came to my support, but everyone deserted me' (2 Timothy 4:16) and 'everyone in the province of Asia has deserted me' (2 Timothy 1:15).

The Lord Jesus knew He would suffer in the same way when He said to His disciples, 'You will all fall away, for it is written, I will strike the shepherd and the sheep will be scattered' (Mark 14:27).

Those who serve the Lord in positions of leadership must consider, and be prepared to meet, if necessary, the cost of physical and emotional suffering.

5.3 Leadership rewards

Although there is a potential cost involved in Christian leadership, there are also significant rewards. These are not the passing rewards of human admiration and status, but the lasting benefits of maturing in the Christian faith and, when the Chief Shepherd appears, receiving a crown of glory that will never fade away (1 Peter 5:4).

The apostle Paul told Timothy, 'Those who have served well gain an excellent standing and great assurance in their faith in Christ Jesus' (1 Timothy 3:13). This is because those who serve are exposed to situations that put their faith to the test. The trials of leadership force Christian leaders to rely more on the Lord Jesus Christ, and, as a result, their faith will be proved genuine (1 Peter 1:6,7). This is true of all Christian experience, faith is made real through works of service. Consequently, those who serve the Lord well through Christian leadership not only look forward to a crown of glory in the life to come but also receive assurance of their faith in this life.

Christian leaders are further entitled to certain benefits from those in their care.

(a) Honour

'The elders who direct the affairs of the church well are worthy of double honour, especially those whose work is preaching and teaching' (1 Timothy 5:17). 'Now we ask you, brothers, to respect those who work hard among you, who are over you in the Lord and who admonish you. Hold them in the highest regard in love because of their work' (1 Thessalonians 5:12,13).

(b) Maintenance

'Don't you know that those who work in the temple get their food from the temple, and those who serve at the altar share in what is offered on the altar? In the same way the Lord has commanded that those who preach the gospel should receive their living from the gospel' (1 Corinthians 9:13,14). 'Anyone who receives instruction in the word must share all good things with his instructor' (Galatians 6:6).

(c) Freedom from trifling accusations

'Do not entertain an accusation against an elder unless it is brought by two or three witnesses' (1 Timothy 5:19).

So, we have seen that there are many rewards for those who serve as Christian leaders, but it should not be forgotten that, as faithful stewards, those who have a talent are obligated to use it in the Lord's service. The apostle Paul expressed this to the Corinthians when he wrote 'Woe to me if I do not preach the gospel: If I preach voluntarily, I have a reward; if not voluntarily, I am simply discharging the trust committed to me' (1 Corinthians 9:16,17).

6 Responsibilities of Christians towards their Leaders

6.1 Election and employment of Christian leaders

We have seen that the Scriptures contain guidance as to the necessary attributes of a Christian leader. However, the situation is not so clear when we come to the mechanics of appointing Christian leaders.

Many evangelical churches model their selection processes on the choosing of the seven leaders recorded in Acts 6. On that occasion the twelve apostles called all the disciples together and told them to choose seven men 'known to be full of the Spirit and wisdom.' The seven were then chosen and presented to the apostles 'who prayed and laid their hands on them' (Acts 6:1-7). It is not recorded as to how the disciples chose the seven, but, in many churches, this is interpreted by the need for all *church members* to vote.

For this method of selection to be effective, it requires each voting member to be well acquainted with the individuals concerned and with the Scriptural guidelines for selecting leaders. This places a responsibility on each member of the church who takes part in the selection process. There are also practical problems in many Christian congregations of deciding who is eligible to vote and what sort of majority is required to make a decision.

An alternative approach is for the existing leaders to be responsible for appointing new leaders. An example of this in Scripture would be the position of Titus in Crete. The apostle Paul, writing to Titus, states, 'The reason I left you in Crete was that you might straighten out what was left unfinished and appoint elders in every town, as I directed you' (Titus 1:5).

It has become traditional that a group of believers forming themselves together as a congregation will have one leader who is on a full-time basis and is effectively employed by the congregation. This has the advantages that there is a focal point for organising the work of the congregation and that increased human resources are brought to bear on the work of the congregation. It is Scriptural, as we have noted, that a Christian leader should receive a material remuneration for his work on behalf of the congregation. However, is it necessarily always a good thing for one of the leaders to be full-time? The apostle Paul made a point of working to supply his own needs (Acts 20:34) and there are a number of potential pitfalls with a full-time pastor.

(a) Christians should all share in the work of the Church through their membership of the Body of Christ. Where a full-time pastor exists there can be a tendency for the congregation to 'delegate' all the 'spiritual' work to the pastor, such that he is expected to do all the preaching, teaching, visiting of the sick etc. This leads to lack of growth for individual believers whose talents in these areas remain unused.

(b) We have seen that responsibility for the congregation rests with the elders or overseers. However, if one of the elders is a full-time pastor, the other elders can become relegated to a role under the supervision of the pastor due to their comparative lack of involvement with the congregation.

This is not to say that the elders should not seek to employ Christians to further the work of their congregation, or that a Christian with a particular talent for teaching or evangelism should not be supported by the congregation. However, they must be careful not to abrogate their authority, nor to allow all the works, necessary for individual spiritual growth, to be undertaken by one man alone.

Similarly, individual members of the congregation have a responsibility to ensure that they remain fully involved in the work of the congregation, using their talents to build each other up in love.

6.2 Submission to Christian leaders

Hebrews 13:17 contains the instruction, 'Obey your leaders and submit to their authority.' The individual Christian is therefore under an obligation to submit to Christian leaders. However, in this age the believer has an additional responsibility in that he or she has to choose, from the wide selection available, which leader to obey or, to look at it another way, which congregation to *join*.

The roots of present day sectarianism were evident in the early church, as we can tell from the Corinthian epistles. In a modern setting the troubles at Corinth would involve walking down the main street of the town and finding the 'Apollos Church', and, on the opposite side of the road, the 'Church of Paul the Apostle' and, further on down the street the 'True Church of Christ.' Today, the situation is worse in that there are many more than three denominations in any locality. There is no such group meeting as *the local Church* but in any area there exists a wide selection of sectarian groups of Christians, each with their own leaders.

Now, the individual believer may primarily be motivated by doctrinal reasons in choosing a congregation to join or become involved with, but he or she must also bear in mind their responsibility to submit to the authority of the leaders of that congregation. If a congregation has leaders who do not conform to the pattern that we have seen in the Scriptures, it would be wrong to submit to the authority of those leaders.

This is a great responsibility for the individual Christian and one that requires much prayerful consideration. The two extremes of blind obedience and spiritual anarchy must be equally avoided. It would be wrong to opt out of the Christian community entirely because of the poor quality of the leadership of a local congregation. Those congregations where the leaders fail to carry out their responsibilities before the Lord must eventually crumble and die, but the Lord will raise up new channels for His service with Christian leaders worthy of the submission of their fellow believers.

6.3 Prayer and encouragement

The apostle Paul instructed Timothy 'I urge then, first of all, that requests, prayers, intercession and thanksgiving be made for everyone —

for kings and all those in authority' (1 Timothy 2:1,2). How much more, then, does this apply to the responsibility of Christians to remember their own leaders in prayer. There is a need to pray not just for wisdom for Christian leaders but also for their preservation under the increased temptations that will befall them.

Also, as with any believer, a Christian leader needs the fellowship and encouragement of his fellow Christians. This involves not only the occasional word of encouragement but practical works of hospitality. Christian leaders are not a separate body but just some of the ligaments helping to support the whole body (Colossians 2:19) and, as such, they too need the support of their fellow members of the Body of Christ, as we all strive to serve our beloved Lord and Saviour, Jesus Christ.

> 'It was He who gave some to be apostles some to be prophets, some to be evangelists, and some to be pastors and teachers, to prepare God's people for works of service, so that the Body of Christ may be built up until we all reach unity in the faith and in the knowledge of the Son of God and become mature, attaining to the whole measure of the fulness of Christ.
>
> Then we will no longer be infants, tossed back and forth by the waves, and blown here and there by every wind of teaching and by the cunning and craftiness of men in their deceitful scheming. Instead, speaking the truth in love, we will in all things grow up into Him Who is the Head, that is Christ. From Him the whole body, joined and held together by every supporting ligament, grows and builds itself up in love, as each part does its work.' (Ephesians 4:11-16).